Journal One

Seasons of Hope

M. Donna MacLeod

AVE MARIA PRESS AVE Notre Dame, Indiana

To Erynne Lee MacLeod,
a cherished daughter who loved Jesus
and now lives with him,
and
to her dad, my dear husband Bryan,
who has faithfully been by my side
every step of this life-giving ministry.

Founded in 1865, Ave Maria Press is a ministry of the United States Province of Holy Cross.

www.avemariapress.com

Paperback: ISBN-13 978-1-64680-233-3

E-book: ISBN-13 978-1-64680-277-7

Cover and text design by Katherine Robinson.

Printed and bound in the United States of America.

Contents

The Seasons of Hope Prayer can be easily found on the back cover of this book.

Welcome to
Seasons of Hope Journal One

Dear Brothers and Sisters in Christ Jesus,

When your loved one went home to the Lord, did you think that God was calling you to a new life in him, too? And that this new life held much more than pain and sorrow?

I had no idea what lay ahead when my daughter Erynne died. Years of caring for the dying and their families as a nurse did not prepare me for my own grief. Yet God would use the lessons I learned for the good of others. From the loss of a precious child, a Christ-centered ministry to the bereaved and a hospice were born. God plans ahead. He didn't forget me, my family, or my community, and he hasn't forgotten you. He wants to console you.

Trusting in God and opening your mind and soul to the Seasons of Hope program blesses you in untold ways. Your broken heart will start to mend as your spirit lifts. I've seen it happen time and again.

Perhaps this *Journal* reached you through the kindness of a concerned friend who knew its mini-retreats with Jesus could ease your sorrow. Or maybe you found all four of the program journals on your own and plan to use them each day or once a week until the sessions are finished. Or you may have wanted to attend a Seasons of Hope group at church but couldn't, so someone from the ministry team sent you a *Journal* and possibly offered to call you each week to support your efforts.

Most likely, though, you have this *Journal* because you joined a Seasons of Hope group that meets at church or online. You might be attending for the first time. Or you might have a season or two under your belt and are back for more. You realize that the support of others who know what you are going through will once more bless your grief journey with God's gift of love.

Whether you use the *Journals* independently or have group support, you are a vital part of this powerful ministry. Grounded in scripture and the healing wisdom, traditions, and practices of the Catholic Church, Seasons of Hope truly focuses on faith and the spiritual side of grieving. In the midst of suffering, it can draw you ever closer to the Lord. What a gift from heaven that is!

A *Journal* and a Bible are all you need for group sessions or independent journaling. You begin each week with the Seasons of Hope Prayer, located on the back cover of this *Journal*. Then you turn to a new Guidepost page for the title, theme, and scripture citation to locate the Bible passage that guides the session. On the next page you will find the Marking the Route activity that draws from the scripture's theme. The adjoining Notes page has space to write your thoughts related to the exercise.

If you attend a group, the facilitator will have faith-sharing questions based on the session's scripture story for you and the other participants to consider. And you also enrich your weekly journey with the *Journal*'s Soul Work that you do at home after the session.

If you are a journaler, you read the session's Bible story and do the Marking the Route exercises plus soothe the wounds of your heart and soul with the Soul Work. The process generally takes about twenty minutes, a commitment that most schedules can handle.

The Soul Work's theme and opening comments in Looking Back offer a fresh way to view the scripture story. You then ask for guidance in A Prayer to Find the Way. You will read Steps along the Path to learn how the scripture story relates to mourning and then spend time with the Reflection section to consider your situation. You can write your thoughts in the space provided under the heading Journal Entry.

To help you cope, Moving Forward offers a Church tradition or act of charity that generates hope. You finish the Soul Work with the Closing Prayer to thank God for the gift of consolation.

The appendix at the end of the booklet has some treasures of its own. Are you interested in literature and websites about losing a loved one? Check out Helpful Resources, which also includes links to sacred images used for contemplation in some sessions. Are you in a group? Use the Network Directory to record contact information about your new friends in Christ. How about ground rules for the group? That's covered in the Guide to Group Etiquette. Want to help your facilitators plan for the next season? The Season Survey lets you formally share your ideas.

By using this *Seasons of Hope Journal One*, you bring the trials of your loss to the Lord. You embrace his teachings, reflect on your loss, and share the painful moments so that your wounded spirit can grow strong in him.

May Seasons of Hope's unique way of placing Jesus Christ at the center of your grief bring you consolation and healing.

In Christ our Hope,
M. Donna MacLeod

Session 1

Guidepost: Point of Departure

Theme: For Whom Are You Looking?

Scripture: John 20:11–18

Marking the Route

Exercise:

Begin your faith story by completing these statements in your own words:

- My name is _____.

- My departed loved one's name is _____.

- His/her death happened _____ weeks/months/years ago.

- The cause of death was . . .

- When he/she died, I was at . . .

- My fondest memory of _____ is . . .

Notes

Soul Work: Point of Departure

Looking Back: *Why Are You Weeping?*

This week we focus on the passage of John 20:11–18 in which Mary Magdalene is asked why she is weeping. The angels in white who are stationed where the body of Jesus had been laid are the first to pose the question to her. Her reply is simple. The Lord has been taken away, and she doesn't know where he is. She is upset! The next moment a question about her weeping comes from the lips of her beloved Jesus. The question reveals his presence to her, but his words focus on her reaction. He knows she believes in him and his promise of everlasting life. Does he also want her to understand her grief?

We, too, face the challenge of our grief when a loved one dies. We cannot bring our dearly departed back from the tomb. We must go on. Some of us weep openly. Some of us hold back the tears. Actually, weeping can be therapeutic. Scientists say that tears contain chemical by-products of stress and can help release emotion. In essence, tears are God's gift to us in our time of mourning.

A Prayer to Find the Way

O divine Savior,
you are with me
at my loved one's tomb.
Darkness surrounds me,
but you see my tears—
even the ones that hide inside me.
You feel my pain.
You know why I weep.
Someday you will wipe away
every last tear.
Help me find my way out
of this tomb of sadness.
Amen.

Steps along the Path

Weeping is one way your inner emotions find expression. Your spectrum of feelings is as vast and unique as those that overwhelmed Mary Magdalene at the tomb. Scripture only hints at her relationship with Jesus, but it was those closest to him who were present on Calvary. As with Mary Magdalene, what you feel depends on what the loss of the deceased means to your life.

Reflection

Take a few moments to look at a photograph that shows happier times with the one you mourn. Consider the uplifting emotion you experienced together back then. Savor that feeling once again.

Journal Entry

It also helps to name the feelings of loss. The act of writing can move the emotion from inside you to the paper. It gives you something to look at. Often it helps you put into words what you find difficult to speak.

To get started, imagine the tomb scene in the scripture story. What might transpire if you were looking for your loved one and Jesus was watching you? Write down what you would tell Jesus about your grief. If you need help, consider these opening phrases:

Lord, losing _____ makes me feel . . .

My connection to _____ that I miss the most is . . .

Moving Forward

Jesus is linked with light in the scriptures (Jn 8:12) and the Creed. The Church gives us a symbol of the risen Christ in the paschal candle, which is usually lit near the coffin (or cremated remains) at the funeral Mass. Did you know that it is a sign of hope?

As a sign of hope in these days of mourning, consider lighting a votive candle in memory of your departed loved one. Honor him or her with a prayer of gratitude to God for your time together. You might place the candle near a picture of happier times or light a candle at your church.

Closing Prayer

Almighty God,
let the grace of my time with you
refresh my heart and soul this week
and lead me from the tomb of my
sadness.
Grant this through Christ our Lord.
Amen.

Session 2

Guidepost: Path to Understanding

Theme: Our Source of Consolation

Scripture: Matthew 11:28–30

Marking the Route

Exercise:
Jesus invites us to draw near to him as a way of coping with our burdens, but he never intrudes. We must go to him. Need a lift? Try this writing exercise.

List three things that make you weary during this period of mourning. Then jot down an example of a time when you sought and received Jesus's help with one of those burdens.

Notes

Soul Work: Path to Understanding

Looking Back: *Our Source of Consolation*

This week's passage (Mt 11:28–30) reveals Jesus's prescription for us when we are weary and burdened. We are to come to him. He knows that the grieving process can sap our energy, leaving us exhausted. It takes mental and emotional effort to recover. Psychologists often refer to this as grief work.

Jesus promises rest. Yet what might rest be? Feeling relaxed enough to fall asleep? Undisturbed slumber? Or does his promise of rest mean peace of mind or spirit?

A plan of action also appears in the passage. Jesus invites us to walk with him and share the yoke he carries to learn his meek and humble ways. When he becomes our guide, grief takes on new meaning. To be meek means to endure loss with patience and without resentment. To act humbly is to proceed in a spirit of respect for the ways of God. Under Jesus's gentle care, we are not alone.

A Prayer to Find the Way

O loving God,
I bring you the burden of my sorrow.
The pain of my grief
is sometimes too much for me.
I ask, in the name of Jesus,
to learn the loving lessons
of your plan
and to be consoled by the good
that flows from it.
Amen.

Steps along the Path

To console means to lessen grief or one's sense of loss. Jesus consoles us through Church traditions. Some parishes let family members select funeral readings, music, and altar flowers; act as lectors, Eucharistic ministers, altar servers, or pallbearers; or offer words of remembrance. These can aid the grieving process.

Our funeral rites celebrate a loved one's life and often bring us comfort. Going forward for Communion at the funeral Mass is a powerful way to reply to Jesus's invitation to come to him. Our "Amen" when we receive the Eucharist testifies that we believe in him.

The Lord doesn't want us to forget our beloved dead. The Church encourages us to honor their eternal souls through prayer, the Communion of Saints, and in a special way during the Feasts of All Saints and All Souls each November.

Reflection

Think about the time around the wake and funeral of your loved one. Try to remember someone who lightened your burden in some way. What did the person say or do that lifted your spirit? Dwell on the gift you received. Did it seem like a gift then? Do you remember another example of kindness?

Journal Entry

Sometimes on the grief journey, it might seem like your feelings get stuck in a rut. Observers might tell you that time heals everything. Those who have been down this road know better: only God heals. You have the difficult job of enduring your loss with patience.

In the space that follows, tell the Lord what burdens you today. Let him into your struggle and be open to his loving plan for you.

Moving Forward

Consider putting down your bundle of grief for a while to reach out to someone in need. Does a friend want to get you out of the house? Remember that they still need you. If conversation is beyond you, send a note or an email to let the person know you're having a good day. Or lend a hand to someone who is hurting. Carry the yoke with that person, and you may gain a new perspective on your own grief journey.

Closing Prayer

O loving God,
the burden of my sorrow
seems to lift somewhat
when I walk closely with Jesus.
He is with those who are hurting
and those who try to ease my sorrow.
Thank you for making me more aware.
Amen.

Session 3

Guidepost: Obstacles on the Journey

Theme: Shattered Dreams

Scripture: Jeremiah 18:1–6

Marking the Route

Exercise:

Most of us don't understand what life without our loved one will be like before he or she dies. But eventually we realize that our hopes and dreams of a future with the deceased are gone, shattered like a precious piece of pottery that falls from its shelf.

Think about a dream that you had for your loved one that never came to be and left you in need of the healing touch of the Lord. How might you honor that dream in the future? If you want to, jot down your thoughts.

Notes

Soul Work: Obstacles on the Journey

Looking Back: *Picking Up the Pieces*

In this session, we use Jeremiah 18:1–6 to explore unfulfilled dreams about our loved ones. The symbols in the passage also help us examine the grief experience.

Mourning can leave us so drained that we feel like inert lumps of clay on a potter's wheel. In difficult moments, the world seems to spin like that wheel. Yet, Jeremiah's image reveals another possibility: God the potter actually uses the swift rotation of the wheel to mold clay into an earthen vessel. A new creation comes to be because of his patient guidance. The scene reminds us that we are in God's hands in any situation, even during mourning.

The Lord wants to make each of us into a new object. The only question is, Will we let him?

A Prayer to Find the Way

O loving God,
how easily I forget
that you are the creator of life,
the giver of my past, present,
and future.
I ask, in the name of Jesus,
to be as supple as clay in your hands.
Let me yield to your gentle touch
and discover new meaning in my life.
Amen.

Steps along the Path

In the fast pace of today's world, not many of us go to a potter's shop to watch an artisan create a piece that we might buy. We usually shop in a store that has finished products, missing out on the ancient process that makes a piece truly special.

Sometimes we handle grief in the same manner. We would rather avoid the workshop where the clay of the soul is stretched, molded, and forced into a useful shape. Who wants to wait while the clay dries or the kiln's fire (grief's pain) toughens it? Until we appreciate our grief and how God uses it to transform us, we stay in sadness like a lifeless lump of clay.

Reflection

Imagine finding a clay pot that slipped off a garden shelf and now lies shattered on the ground. Suppose someone had made the pot for you, and you treasure it. What might you feel when you find it? Would you try to put it back together again?

Journal Entry

Some of us use the word "brokenhearted" to describe losing someone dear. The pain can be so strong that we feel it physically as an ache in the chest or a sensation of emptiness as if our heart had shattered and left a void. Sometimes, numbness overtakes us. We may even feel betrayed by others, the deceased, or God.

Write about your feelings. No matter how far along you are on the grief journey, seek the Lord's gentle touch to transform you into the work of art he wants you to become.

Moving Forward

If you long to be as flexible as clay in the Potter's hands, spend time with the Blessed Sacrament. Besides mindfully receiving Communion, you could visit the tabernacle or chapel of reservation and attend Eucharistic Adoration.

In the quiet of the church or chapel, shut out the world and your thoughts and share your brokenness with the one who truly can put life's pieces back together again. Open your heart. Ask the Holy Spirit to guide your time there so that mending can begin.

Closing Prayer

O gentle Savior,
the brokenness of my life
brings sorrow and pain,
but your love can heal my heart.
I give you thanks
for touching my shattered dreams
and helping me find consolation.
Amen.

Session 4

Guidepost: Path to Inner Healing

Theme: Finding Joy

Scripture: John 16:19–24

Marking the Route

Exercise:

Since your loss, have you ever wondered whether joy will be yours again? It's a concern that often goes unspoken during mourning. Consider what might help you find joy again, especially those things that haven't found a place in your prayers. Then write a letter to God in the space below. Ask for whatever would rekindle your joy.

Notes

Soul Work: Path to Inner Healing

Looking Back: *Finding Joy*

In John 16:19–24, we hear Jesus's words of encouragement for his followers. He knows that they don't understand that his time on earth is ending. The disciples are like the rest of us who cannot imagine life without a loved one when he or she is still alive.

Jesus addresses the disciples' anxiety about being left behind. He knows that they, like us, will not be happy in the throes of grief. Responding to their questions about being separated from him, he explains that, in the end, they will ask nothing of him. The problem is that they haven't approached the Father with their troubles. If they would pray in the name of the Son, their grief would become joy.

To use the name of Jesus suggests an intimate relationship with him. If we are in sync with the Lord, we appreciate his ways. Since he wants us to find joy again, why not seek it through prayer?

A Prayer to Find the Way

O God the Father,
I ask for guidance
on this walk of sorrow.
Jesus gave us new life
through his Death and Resurrection
and promised that those who mourn
will find joy again.
I ask in his name to be open
to the peace and joy
that you send
through the Holy Spirit.
Amen.

Steps along the Path

For some, joy is rooted in what the world offers. It is an emotion evoked by well-being, success, good fortune, or the prospect of possessing what one desires. Scripture, however, reveals that joy is a gift from God, a fruit of the Holy Spirit that is always available to us (Gal 5:22). So why aren't we happy all the time?

Others may wish we were cheerful, but experiencing the pain of loss is important. When we're consumed with sorrow, however, it may become difficult to accept help or think a happy thought. We must work through the grieving process to be healed. As with any gift, we must be ready to accept joy.

Can we find moments of joy amid sadness? Jesus tells us it is possible! Seek God's help in his name. The Holy Spirit, the master of prayer, will intercede.

Reflection

Think about one aspect of life that brought you the most joy in the past. Was your deceased loved one part of the experience? Did you recognize God's hand in your happiness?

Journal Entry

If you are like the average mourner, the time will come when your mind shifts away from sad thoughts. Your sense of relief may last only a minute or two at first, but it shows that you are on the mend. Eventually, something about your loved one will come to mind and you won't choke up with sadness. In fact, you may even smile at the memory.

Jot down a quality of your loved one that brought you joy. Explain to the Lord how you will use what your loved one taught you.

Moving Forward

Each year, the Church brings us back to Calvary on Good Friday. If we take the journey to heart, we experience the darkness of grief. The altar is stripped bare, and Mass is not celebrated as we fast and wait for Easter, when alleluias once again fill the air. Jesus's Resurrection is a story of joy.

This week, find something to rejoice about. You might connect with a friend from the past or simply savor the smile of a child. Whatever you discover, rejoice and be glad.

Closing Prayer

O loving God,
sometimes the darkness of my grief
makes it hard to welcome joy.
Jesus wants my joy to be complete,
and I am grateful for that.
Thank you for showing the way.
Amen.

Session 5

Guidepost: Way of Suffering

Theme: The Way of the Cross

Scripture: Luke 23:13–56

Marking the Route

Exercise:

Contemplate the Passion of Christ by viewing the Stations of the Cross as though you were there among the crowd. This ancient tradition is a powerful way to pray and grow closer to the Lord in spirit. It can open our hearts to his love and consolation.

Identify which station shows the kind of suffering or sorrow you currently experience. Jot down your thoughts.

The traditional stations are as follows:

1. Jesus Is Condemned
2. Jesus Takes Up His Cross
3. The First Fall
4. Jesus Meets His Mother
5. Simon of Cyrene Helps Jesus
6. Veronica Wipes the Face of Jesus
7. Jesus Falls a Second Time
8. Jesus Speaks to the Women
9. Jesus Falls a Third Time
10. Jesus Is Stripped of His Clothing
11. Jesus Is Nailed to the Cross
12. Jesus Dies on the Cross
13. Jesus Is Taken Down from the Cross
14. Jesus Is Laid in the Tomb

You can find a link to images of the Stations of the Cross in the appendix under Helpful Resources (see "Sacred Images").

Note: Next week, have a favorite picture of your loved one with you for the session.

Notes

Soul Work: Way of Suffering

Looking Back: *Bearing Your Cross*

I n this session, we reflect on the Way of the Cross, envisioning our own walk of sorrow in the shadow of Jesus's Passion. We also read Luke 23:13–56. Yet reading about Jesus's suffering is not the same as bearing his Cross.

So it is when you vigil with someone who is dying a painful death. Your heart goes out to your loved one, but you cannot absorb his or her pain. You can only be present to the other's distress and the emotions that stir within you.

Compassion is a gift that unites us to each other. When you view the suffering and Crucifixion of Christ with compassion, you realize he knows how you feel in times of sorrow. Knowing he is with you can give you the courage to bear your own pain.

A Prayer to Find the Way

Lord Jesus,
you accepted the cross of suffering
for us
and took the weight of the world
upon your shoulders.
You stumbled on the way to Calvary
but trusted God's plan.
Help me embrace my cross of sorrow
and trust that good will come from it.
Amen.

Steps along the Path

The Cross of Christ is the sign of the Christian. In Jesus's day, crucifixion was horrific punishment for slaves or non-Roman citizens convicted of grave crimes. Jesus's death on the Cross made it a sacred symbol of his Passion as well as a sign of protection and defense for his followers.

Early Christian worship included the Cross. The gesture of forming a cross on the forehead with the right thumb signified unity with Jesus. At the beginning of Lent each year, blessed ashes are traced in a cross on the foreheads of the faithful. The mark of ashes reminds us of our own mortality and tells the world that we believe in Jesus Christ, a Savior who embraces suffering and forever elevates its meaning.

Reflection

Find some quiet time at home, at church, or outdoors to gaze upon a cross that brings Jesus to mind. Consider what the Cross of Christ meant in the life of your departed loved one. Ponder what it has meant to you in the past. What is its meaning now?

Journal Entry

Jesus expects his followers to take up whatever cross life gives to us. To bear your cross means that you hold it up, support its weight, and move forward with it. He doesn't ask you to lead the way but simply to follow him. On his ascent to Mount Calvary, he struggled with the weight of his Cross but somehow found the strength and courage to continue.

Write to Jesus and share with him the times you have stumbled and fallen as you have borne the cross of mourning.

Moving Forward

The ancient tradition of signing the cross with the right thumb on the forehead is done at Mass at the gospel reading and also involves signing over the lips and heart. More often, we trace the cross with our hand from forehead to waist and then from the left to right shoulder to name the Holy Trinity in the briefest of prayers.

This week, each time you make the Sign of the Cross, pause at each motion and mindfully recite the name of the assigned Divine Person—Father, Son, or Holy Spirit—remembering with "Amen" that the Sign of the Cross blesses.

Closing Prayer

Lord Jesus,
in your Cross I find consolation
for my grief.
Your strength and courage
sustain me.
Through you I discover the Father
and the Holy Spirit.
I am forever grateful.
Amen.

Session 6

Guidepost: Final Destination

Theme: Untie Him

Scripture: John 11:1–44

Marking the Route

Exercise (for a group member):
Show the group a picture of your departed loved one and tell why the photo or setting is a favorite of yours.

Exercise (for a journaler):
At each session, you have honored your deceased loved one with word and prayer. Today, go a step further. Look at a picture of your departed loved one and write down why this photo or setting is a favorite of yours.

Note: Seasons of Hope *has four different seasons. Find out when the next one starts.*

Notes

Soul Work: Final Destination

Looking Back: *Letting God*

T his session's passage about the raising of Lazarus (Jn 11:1–44) reveals common responses to losing a loved one and demonstrates how God can turn a tragic situation into one of triumph.

We sense that Martha and Mary are trusted friends who have great faith in Jesus. They know how to get a message to him while he is avoiding the authorities. The sisters must realize that Jesus is in danger, but they want him to save Lazarus.

Scripture shows that Jesus knows the urgency of his friend's illness but doesn't rush to his aid. He waits—a response we often get when we pray for help in our struggles.

When Jesus approaches Bethany after Lazarus has died, Martha meets him outside the village. Instead of being grateful that he has risked his life for them, she scolds him for not arriving sooner. The Son of God has chosen his own approach to help Lazarus, and Martha feels betrayed. Like so many of us in similar circumstances, she believes that her plan is better.

A Prayer to Find the Way

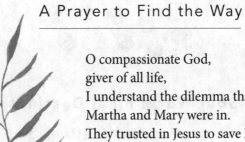

O compassionate God,
giver of all life,
I understand the dilemma that
Martha and Mary were in.
They trusted in Jesus to save Lazarus,
yet death came.
I ask, in the name of your Son,
to truly trust in your benevolence
in these difficult days.
Amen.

Steps along the Path

Imagine standing face-to-face with Jesus as Martha did outside the village. After blurting out her feelings of betrayal, she confesses that she wants him to pray to God for her brother because God will listen to him!

When you wonder if God is listening, remember Martha. She also wondered, and she went on to sainthood.

Reflection

Jesus stayed outside the village and did not go to the tomb to raise Lazarus, but Martha didn't give up. She went to her sister and told Mary that Jesus had asked for her. When Mary fell at Jesus's feet weeping, he was moved to tears.

Think about those tears. If you were at Jesus's feet weeping in grief, what might his tears tell you?

Journal Entry

When Jesus, the sisters of Lazarus, and the crowd arrived at the tomb, Martha spoke up again. Jesus wanted the stone removed from the cave entrance to show the glory of God. Martha complained there would be a stench.

Think about your reaction after your loved one passed on. Then answer the following questions:

What were your complaints? Share them with God. (If you had none, share why you felt positive.)

How has God touched your loss?

Moving Forward

Death has a stench, but it is believed that God's presence brings a pleasant fragrance. The Church uses incense to heighten awareness of God's presence during the funeral Mass. Aromatic gum and spices are burned, giving off soft whirls of perfumed smoke that seem to carry our prayers to heaven.

This week use incense to adore God, who gives everlasting life to you and your departed loved one. As you watch the smoke rise, inhale the pleasant scent and offer a prayer to the Almighty. If you don't have incense, let the following prayer lift your mind and broken heart to God.

Closing Prayer

O God of all blessings,
thank you for the gift
of special people in my life
and for the comfort of knowing
that heaven awaits us
through your Son.
May the sweet fragrance of your love
surround my departed loved ones.
Amen.

Appendix

Helpful Resources

Books

DeLorenzo, Leonard J. *Our Faithful Departed: Where They Are and Why It Matters.* Notre Dame, IN: Ave Maria Press, 2022.

Gilbert, Richard B. *Finding Your Way After Your Parent Dies: Hope for Grieving Adults.* Notre Dame, IN: Ave Maria Press, 1999.

Helping Children Cope with Death. Portland: Dougy Center, 2015.

Helping Teens Cope with Death. Portland: Dougy Center, 2015.

Hickman, Martha Whitmore. *Healing After Loss: Daily Meditations for Working Through Grief.* New York: Avon Books, 1994.

Kübler-Ross, Elisabeth, and David Kessler. *On Grief and Grieving: Finding the Meaning of Grief through the Five Stages of Loss.* New York: Scribner, 2005.

Lafser, Christine O'Keeffe. *An Empty Cradle, a Full Heart: Reflections for Mothers and Fathers after Miscarriage, Stillbirth, or Infant Death.* Chicago: Loyola Press, 1998.

Noel, Brook, and Pamela D. Blair. *I Wasn't Ready to Say Goodbye: Surviving, Coping, and Healing after the Sudden Death of a Loved One.* Updated ed. Naperville, IL: Sourcebooks, 2008.

Nouwen, Henri J. M. *Turn My Mourning into Dancing: Finding Hope in Hard Times.* Nashville: Thomas Nelson, 2001.

O'Connor, Mary-Frances. *The Grieving Brain: The Surprising Science of How We Learn from Love and Loss.* New York: Harper One, 2022.

O'Hearn, Patrick, Bryan Feger, Kelly and Ryan Breaux. *The Grief of Dads: Support and Hope for Catholic Fathers Navigating Child Loss.* Notre Dame, IN: Ave Maria Press, 2023.

Roe, Gary. *Comfort for the Grieving Parent's Heart: Hope and Healing After Losing Your Child.* Cleveland: Healing Resources, 2020.

Rowland, Joanna. *The Memory Box: A Book about Grief.* Illustrations by Thea Baker. Minneapolis: Sparkhouse Family, 2017.

Rupp, Joyce. *Now That You've Gone Home: Courage and Comfort for Times of Grief.* Notre Dame, IN: Ave Maria Press, 2009.

Shoener, Ed, and John P. Dolan, eds. *When a Loved One Dies by Suicide: Comfort, Hope, and Healing for Grieving Catholics.* Notre Dame, IN: Ave Maria Press, 2020.

Tighe, Tommy. *St. Dymphna's Playbook: A Catholic Guide to Finding Mental and Emotional Well-Being.* Notre Dame, IN: Ave Maria Press, 2021.

White, Michael, and Tom Corcoran. *Seriously, God? Making Sense of Life Not Making Sense.* Notre Dame, IN: Ave Maria Press, 2021.

Wolfelt, Alan D. *Understanding Your Grief: Ten Essential Touchstones for Finding Hope and Healing Your Heart.* Fort Collins, CO: Companion Press, 2021.

Zonnebelt-Smeenge, Susan J., and Robert C. De Vries. *Getting to the Other Side of Grief: Overcoming the Loss of a Spouse.* Grand Rapids, MI: Baker Books, 2019.

Websites

www.usccb.org/bible provides free access to the New American Bible.

www.hospicefoundation.org has a treasure trove of articles on grief and grieving.

www.whatsyourgrief.com offers grief and bereavement education and social media resources for adults, teens, and children.

www.widowedparent.org supports widowed mothers and fathers with children in the home.

www.avemariapress.com has books on prayer, bereavement, and spiritual enrichment.

www.compassionatefriends.org offers information and support for families who lose a child.

www.grasphelp.org supports those who have lost a loved one through the misuse of drugs.

www.healgrief.org provides grief resources, virtual groups, educational programs, and a map to find local and national support.

www.samaritanshope.org links to information on suicide-survivor issues for all ages.

www.taps.org helps those grieving the death of a military loved one by providing free grief resources, including casework, counseling, publications, retreats, seminars, and more.

Sacred Images

"Divine Mercy," www.thedivinemercy.org/message.

"Rosary," https://rosarycenter.org/how-to-pray-the-rosary.

"Sacred Heart of Jesus," https://m.theholyrosary.org/sacredheart/.

"Stations of the Cross," https://aleteia.org/2018/03/30/pray-the-stations-of-the -cross-with-these-beautiful-images-and-prayers/.

Network Directory

Interacting with others of faith who understand what it means to lose a loved one gives you a chance to give and receive support. Use the space below for contact information of participants in your Seasons of Hope group.

Name_____

Phone number_____

Email_____

Name_____

Phone number_____

Email_____

Name_____

Phone number_____

Email_____

Name_____

Phone number_____

Email_____

Name_____

Phone number_____

Email_____

Name_____

Phone number_____

Email_____

Name_____

Phone number_____

Email_____

Name_____

Phone number_____

Email_____

Name_____

Phone number_____

Email_____

Guide to Group Etiquette

A facilitator guides the faith-sharing process by keeping the focus on the Lord and the session questions. A facilitator doesn't teach, preach, or advise. The facilitator creates a safe place for you to talk about your feelings about loss and receive consolation.

You are expected to

- come each week and make it known if you can't;
- arrive on time;
- treat others with respect;
- share your faith story and then let others talk;
- be a good listener;
- keep what is shared in confidence; and
- be open to God touching you through others.

Don't worry if tears flow. They are part of grieving. Smiles and laughter are welcome, too.

Season Survey

Please take a few moments to complete the statements below about your experience with our Seasons of Hope group. Thank you!

1. I learned about Seasons of Hope from

2. I think the meeting room is

3. For me, the session start time is

4. For me, the length of the weekly sessions is

5. The focus on prayer, scripture, and God is

6. Private time to write, listen to music, or read allows me to

7. I find faith sharing

8. For me, the fellowship break is

9. Soul Work between sessions lets me

10. What I learned from Seasons of Hope is

11. When the next Seasons of Hope group forms, I

12. I'd also like to say

Date: _____

Name (optional): _____

Acknowledgments

How grateful I am to God for the blessing of so many who made this updated edition of the *Seasons of Hope Leader's Guide* and *Journals* possible. Only God can make goodness flow from the sorrow we bear. And I truly believe the Seasons of Hope program embodied in these books is a powerful witness to that reality.

My heartfelt thanks remain with the clergy, family, friends, and bereaved who believed long ago that this work would enrich our parishes. They were right! I'm also grateful to everyone who lifts us up in prayer and to the brokenhearted who trust in the Lord and come to be comforted. I appreciate the priests, deacons, religious sisters and brothers, lay pastoral advisors, and diocesan leaders that welcome the program. And I admire the amazing Seasons of Hope facilitators and helpers, at my side and everywhere else, who have faithfully poured their gifts, talents, and compassion into season after season of this Catholic grief-support ministry. Their feedback is woven into this edition.

The ongoing enthusiasm and expertise of the Ave Maria Press professionals and staff are greatly appreciated. Many thanks especially to Eileen Ponder, Karey Circosta, Erin Pierce, and Stephanie Sibal for championing this new edition.

As always, my husband Bryan's wisdom, love, faith, and generous spirit greatly influenced this work. I treasure the input of our dear daughter Meganne, who remains a constant source of love and support, and the memory of our dear Erynne, whose death opened my heart to all who mourn.

M. Donna MacLeod is a Catholic lay leader and founder of the nationwide Seasons of Hope ministry to the bereaved. She is the author of the bestselling Seasons of Hope program, which includes a leader's guide, four journals, and digital support resources. Her work in grief support was inspired by the loss of her daughter, Erynne, in 1988 and the compassionate response of her parish.

MacLeod earned a bachelor's degree in nursing at Northeastern University in Boston, Massachusetts, and her master's degree in nursing at Boston University. She served as an oncology clinical specialist at several hospitals, an educator, and the director of VNA Hospice of Greater Milford, Massachusetts.

MacLeod is active in leadership at her local parish and speaks across the United States and Canada on grief, loss, and lay ministry. She is a member of the Catholic Family Life Association and serves as a commissioned minister of consolation with the National Catholic Ministry to the Bereaved, where she previously served as a training facilitator and a member of the board of trustees.

MacLeod lives with her husband, Bryan, in the Boston, Massachusetts, area. She can be reached at seasonsofhope35@gmail.com.